poems of the fallen angel

by
Jack E. Hite

DORRANCE & COMPANY
Philadelphia

Copyright © 1971 by Jack E. Hite
All Rights Reserved
ISBN 0-8059-1622-9
Library of Congress Catalog Card Number: 75-173992
Printed in the United States of America

CONTENTS

	Page
The Melody	1
The Fallen Angel	1
The Companion	3
Always Beside Me	5
Roma's Sky	5
The Door	6
The Flower And The Rain	6
Of Passion And Of Love	7
Deliver Me From Hate	8
God's Love	8
The River	9
The Struggle	10
What Is Man?	11
Seeking To Know	12
Searching	13
Many Trials, Many Lives	13
In Your Hands	14
Understand	15
Not Ours To Have	16
Thoughts	17
The Merry-Go-Round	18
The Unknowing Sleep	19
Courage	20
The Pessimist	21
Your Day To Make	21
Look For The Good	22
Silver Sands	23
Sing Us A Song	23
Doubt Not, Fear Not	24
Time	25
Friends	26
Talent	26

Born In Sin?	27
Man's Destiny?	28
To Sleep, To Dream	29
Think	30
Be Thankful	30
The Star	31
The Spirit Of Christmas	32
His Gift Our Gift	33
Be Still	34
War Or Peace	34
The Flag	34
The Land	35
Satan's Song	36
God's Song	37
The Meeting	38
The Fallen Angel Wonders	40
The Awakening	40
The Aquarian Sunrise	41

POEMS OF A FALLEN ANGEL

The Melody

I hear a melody, as if it were floating on the wind.
To catch its fleeting notes, my ear I bend.
But no, it is not riding on the breeze.
Perhaps it is the rustling of the leaves on the trees.

But the leaves, they are quiet and still,
And the music, my mind continues to fill.
I listen close and look around,
But no source for the music can be found.

It is like tiny silver bells quietly ringing,
And joy to my heart I feel it bringing.
It refreshes my soul like a cool clear pool.
Then doubt creeps in and I think I'm a fool.

As I continue to doubt, I hear the music fade,
And I wonder how on earth it ever was made.
I turn around and walk away,
And think my mind with tricks did play.

Time has passed by and I think once more,
Of that beautiful tinkling rhythm, that haunting score.
And now I know to much dismay,
It was the music of my soul and I turned it away.

It was calling me, pleading to be heard,
And I turned my back and thought it absurd
That God was giving to me that day
A chance that comes only once along life's way.

The Fallen Angel

Listen, my children, to you I must speak
Of things you do not know, of things you must seek.
Of hills and valleys of mountains and glens,
Of God and heaven and the stars therein.
Of man, his dreams and his very soul,
Of his struggle, his strife toward some unknown goal.

Man struck out from his father's home,
For in all creation he desired to roam.
He sailed about from star to star,
This child of God, he wandered afar.
He gathered knowledge of all creation,
This spark of God was now full of elation.

Then he came upon a new place
That made him stop and turn his face.
What was that down below?
He knew there were things he did not know.
He then settled himself down upon the land,
To soak up knowledge and know more of the plan.

He watched the creatures with unsurpassed desire,
He did not know that he was playing with fire.
A thought flashed across his celestial mind,
To enter the body of these creatures, that would be fine.
Once inside he thought this was sure bliss,
And for a while his celestial freedom he did not miss.

Then one day when he felt he had no more knowledge to gain,
He desired to go back among the stars again.
Horror then struck and he was filled with pain!
Try as he would he could not leave this earthly plane!
He fell on his face and pleaded to God.
"Come save me," he cried "from this earthly sod!"

God came and told him what he had done,
And shed tears of stardust for his spiritual son.
God then looked upon his pleading soul,
And said, "My son you are not whole.
You have been split one end to the other,
You have lost your half, you must seek another."

God then spoke words of great omen,
"Your other half, my son, will now be woman.
And furthermore," God said to the quaking mortal,
"The road will be difficult back to heaven's portal.
Your other half you must endlessly seek,
And your soul to reunite when one day you meet.

"You will fail and fall far away from me,
For the demands of flesh will overcome thee.
But I will grant you this, my son,
When each of your earthly lives is done,
You will enjoy a great and blissful repast,
In which you can meditate and weigh your earthly past.

"Before you then don a new mortal shell,
You will know what lessons you must learn well.
After many lives you will then start uphill,
Progressing in love and grace, then until
You see the beautiful heavenly light,
And your soul in joy will then reunite.

"Then, my son, you can come home,
And set by me in my heavenly throne.
You will then be among the most wise,
From the knowledge gained in your earthly guise,
And once again you will hear the music of the soul,
As you roam in heaven with those that are whole."

The Companion

In the beginning man drew from himself a being,
To be his companion, to share the creation he was seeing.

Together in happiness they did roam,
For they were free from the flesh in this God-given home.

They were in a state that God had meant,
To study his creation, this earth he had sent.

But there were others who to the earth they came,
And they did not hold to God or his teachings the same.

They took the earth as a playground for themselves to express,
And in mortal flesh their sprits they did dress.

All sorts of fantastic forms they did take,
As the earth, its creation they proceeded to rape.

Now those who were watching the creation in their meant-to-be state,
Knew they must help their brothers who had fallen before it was too late.

They knew they too must enter into the physical plane,
If they were to help their brothers, get them back to God's lane.

They first created a physical being known as man,
Then created woman to beside him stand.

Together these two were one, the whole,
And together they were to play out their God-given role.

They were given a land, a beautiful garden,
Where they were to work, to seek their brothers' pardon.

But they too found that demands of even their perfect flesh were hard to meet.
And before long they too began to stray from God's holy seat.

These sons of God with the sons of man began to mix.
It was not long before this caused the souls in the flesh to fix.

The fall from God was now completely done,
And man could no longer look at his mate and say, "We are one."

For now in the flesh they were torn apart,
And through eons of time each would seek the other with an aching heart.

They struggle in their prison of their mortal shell,
And with only half of their soul they must fight off the demons of hell.

Can man ever regain his heavenly state?
Or is the mortal earth his eternity's fate?

Man can and will return from which he came,
Given time and understanding he will return to the same.

For there are very few of those who do still hold God's intended way,
And are here to help us even in this faraway day.

Always Beside Me

She is always there beside me, there all of the while,
She is always there beside me with her understanding smile.
Though I may be foolish and go way out upon a limb,
She is always there beside me when I decide to come in.

She is always there beside me when things do go wrong,
She is always there beside me helping me to be strong.
Though she may not always agree with the way that I think,
She is always there beside me to fill my missing link.

She is always there beside me and makes my life complete,
She is always there beside me when myself I must meet.
She gives me her love from the very bottom of her heart.
She is always there beside me, "O God, may we never part."

She is always there beside me and places her hand in mine,
She is always there beside me, O! May I be worthy of her for all time.
May I give to her all she has given to me,
And may beside me always, through all eternity she be.

Roma's Sky

I stood and watched that beautiful sky,
With fleecy white clouds that gracefully slid by.

And I wondered why God had gave us beauty so much.
No artist has ever captured this Godly touch.

The fleecy white clouds looked like beds for the angels,
And my thoughts went rampant and my soul did tingle.

Why was I moved by so common a view?
At most any time you can raise your eyes and catch the hue.

I feel it is because we rarely raise our eyes to comprehend,
For we are so full of the dark clouds within.

The Door

The door stands there closed, but it is not locked,
The door stands there for man to open, you need not even knock.

The door stands there with a welcome that none can match,
But so few who pass by bother to try the latch.

Those few who do respond to its beckoning call,
Find it swings open easily, with no effort at all.

As the door swings open and reveals what is inside,
Those who open it stand in amazement and their eyes, too, open wide.

For you see, this door is a mighty portal,
And the understanding inside is meant for every mortal.

These who walk in span man's greatest rift,
And they understand they have been given life's mightiest gift.

That gift is that they now understand
Of themselves, of God, and of their fellow man.

Their mind is now thrown open wide,
And it makes no difference what other men are, they all stand
    side by side.

And as they turn to slowly walk away,
They will notice the door does open stay.

They know now that they may return at will,
As they know there is much more to learn, O so much more still!

They have opened the door that all men must do,
If we are to know what in life is meant for you, for you, and you.

The Flower And The Rain

Said the spring flower to the gently falling rain,
"Thank you oh so kindly for coming that I may bloom again."

Replied the rain to the flower, "It is my desire
To melt the winter's freeze like a gently warming fire.

"So from the now soft earth you may again raise your head,
And announce to the world the end of the cold winter's dread.

"You will now cover the countryside with your blazing beauty,
For every spring it is the message of God we bring, it is our duty.

"If man could only understand the message that we bring.
It is the story of he and God and we bring it every spring.

"Man for oh so long has been in a deep winter's freeze,
And God's love coming down is the spring rain, if you please.

"But man's winter has been long and hard, the freeze very, very deep,
And he hardly notices God's love as down to him it does seep.

"But God's love, like we the rains, will continue to fall,
And the day is coming when He will win, and from the freeze free them all.

"Then man will burst forth in that most wonderful glorious spring,
And his glory, my beautiful flower, will put even you to shame."

Of Passion And Of Love

Of passion and of love, man tends to confuse the two,
Of passion and of love, man is not sure which is true.

Passion man has, for many, many things,
But love seldom does passion ever, ever bring.

For passion is possessive, the filling of man's own desire,
And love is of giving, a giving that man can never, never tire.

Man's desire for passion, for the most, is not the highest kind,
And in his drive to fill his wants, he leaves his better thoughts behind.

Now man will hide his passion under the name of love,
And attempt to fill his wants in the name of God above.

Man will pray to God for wealth, so his love he can express,
Never dreaming the kind of wealth he wants will his love only repress.

For love is plain, simple and so pure,
And must come first, before passion. That is sure.

The line is so fine and hard to ascertain,
That man finds it difficult to avoid passion's pain.

Now passion is that only, of the material realm,
And love is that that comes when God is at the helm.

Deliver Me From Hate

God of my God, deliver me from hate,
Deliver me from this thing that destroys all, before it is too late.

Help me help others, that a way to be free from hate must be found,
Before each of us to this earth, find ourselves in spirit bound.

Now hate is the woe of those that hate,
And of no measure of those hated does it take.

To hate with a vengeful bent
Does sever our soul, and from God we are rent.

Hate seems to be what we must overthrow,
If we are to progress, and from this mortal world we may finally go.

God's Love

If I could only give to you great wisdom in my words,
If I could only express great truths that so few have really heard.

If I could only tell you by the moving of my pen,
The things that are surging, the things I know within.

The things that I believe with all of my heart,
The things that can give to you life with a new start.

For I believe that from God we were truly sent,
And through our folly, ourselves from Him we rent.

I believe that God watches over us every single day,
Hoping to see some small sign we are turning back His way.

I believe that God is radiant with pure, pure love,
And He pours it down upon us from His place above.

But we have built a shell around our soul, you understand,
And His love runs right off of us, as rain runs from the land.

If we could only make in our shell a very tiny crack,
God's great love would filter in and to Him we would start back.

Then this shell of doubt and fear we could cast aside,
And full of God's great love, we would then cease to hide.

The River

God creates a river just like man in his beginning state,
All sparkling clean and pure. This I must relate.

The river is much like man as it wanders on its way,
And the story of its course I will tell you on this day.

The river begins in the mountains, all clean and so pure,
And cascades, oh so gaily as it begins its life's tour.

As it rushes down the mountain it becomes home for fish and trout,
And as it nears the valley floor it feels its importance, beyond any doubt.

It slips into the valley and makes a path as easily as a knife,
And feels full of glory as it gives all around it nourishment for life.

On it goes, bubbling and singing its merry song,
And thinks with too much beauty, what could go wrong?

But the river now, like man, thinks too much of its own deeds,
And the course it is to follow it now fails to heed.

The course back to God and his ocean blue and bright
Seems full of tangles and strikes the river with plight.

Its bed is now full of weeds that badly hamper its flow,
And it swirls around in eddies, not sure which way to go.

It moves along very sluggish, just following the lay of the land,
And dully it hopes God will save it, by His very hand.

But the worst is yet to come for our river friend,
For the filth of the demon man now starts to flow in.

The river cannot resist it and only adds to its woe,
For it has lost the power for filth to overthrow.

It is sure it will now become a damned stagnant pool.
O why did it leave its intended course? Why was it such a fool?

God sees the river's plight and with forgiveness in His heart,
Opens up the heavens and brings pure rain to give it a new start.

The rain fills the river and overflows it banks,
And washes away the filth. The river gives its thanks.

The river surges forward and scours the weeds from its bed,
And with a mighty roar, rushes to God's blue ocean straight ahead.

The Struggle

We have survived upon this earth for thousands and thousands of years,
We have survived upon this earth in spite of our torments and fears.

Ever since our very beginning we have known worry and pain,
And our ever search for peace has always been in vain.

Great ideals have risen and fell,
As man has struggled to save himself from his earthly hell.

In spite of man's well-aimed thoughts,
His progress has been slow, for his own troubles he has wrought.

To be free from war, man on his knees to God does plead,
Then turns around and sows the next war's seed.

Man prays to God for great truths that he may understand,
Then takes those truths and twists them to enhance his earthly stand.

You see, man on this earth is in a rather strange state,
As he struggles with himself to overcome his fate.

All really know the right path to tread,
But to do it they must let their soul guide their head.

For man's soul is very old and very wise,
And of all his earthly dreams and desires only his soul survives.

Man will find peace when he knows all men are the same,
And lets his soul rule, his flesh to tame.

When he realizes each soul is of God a spark,
It will illuminate him and raise him from the dark.

What Is Man?

What is man, is he that of the flesh of the earth?
What is man, is he that with a heart that beats even before birth?

What is man, is he that with a brain with which to think?
What is man, is he that which is a freak of nature, some odd kink?

What is man, is he that which uses tools which he did make?
What is man, is he that which makes weapons to make his fellow man quake?

What is man, is he all of those?
What is man, that above all else he rose?

What is man, that he can love and hate with fiery passion?
What is man, who toward his fellow man can feel compassion?

What is man, who believes that by God he was spawned?
What is man, is he that which is ever seeking the eternal dawn?

What is man, is he that which was given an opportunity above all else?
What is man? He is that which will remain man, until he finds himself.

Seeking To Know

Why must we blindly stumble around,
With no purpose in life that can be found?

Why must we be like a leaf on the wind,
Just tossed about and no goal drive within?

Why do we not for great purposes strive,
To make life worthy instead of a plunging dive?

Why, oh why, are there so precious few,
Who know where they are going and know it true?

Why cannot we each know what we must do,
Then have the courage to pursue it through and through?

Why must we be weak when we have the chance,
To help mankind and their lives to enhance?

Why do we falter and blindly flee,
When only we need to stop and raise our eyes to thee?

Is it only because we fail to understand,
That all things will be given by thy helping hand?

Is it because we think we are so great,
That we need not approach your open gate?

Is it because we have forgotten what we are?
O, God in heaven have we fallen that far!?

We pray to thee to take away what is weak,
That thy great truth we may fully speak.

O God, please help our faltering kind,
That your purpose for us we may truly find.

Searching

Searching, searching, searching our whole life long,
Searching, searching for the eternal dawn.
Searching for that which makes our lives complete,
That will take away our despair and feeling of defeat.

Searching, searching, searching for something we can grab hold,
Searching, searching for the peace we are told.
Searching for life in a perfect state,
That our pains will go and our woes terminate.

Searching, searching, searching that others will us understand,
Searching, searching for someone who will kindly take our hand.
Searching, trying to find a way
That will bring us into focus this very day.

Searching, searching, searching in every direction we can,
Searching, searching, never dreaming the truth is really close at hand.
Searching, wondering why all these things God did hide,
But our searching will end the day we realize it is all with us inside.

Many Trails, Many Lives

If what we are taught is really true,
How few of us must reach heaven's door and pass through.

Can man really in only one span of life
Overcome all evil, all earthly strife?

Will we be able in a lifetime to reach
The perfection that our Lord, he did teach?

Is there one man who can read this and honestly say,
"I have no hates, I love all, I covet not, I'm on my way.

"Because I have no sin my heart is pure,
And all in one lifetime I reached this, I'm sure."

There are those who have most surely reached this state,
But not in one lifetime, this I must relate.

Our experiences upon this earth
Are for our learning, our birth, our rebirth.

And as we pass through life after life,
We go through trials, temptations and strife.

Then if some of our weaknesses we overcome,
We climb the ladder back up, rung by rung.

But if in a life you willfully cause others woe,
Look out, my friend, for the next life you reap what you sow.

God has given to us on this earth the chance,
That in each life our souls we may enhance.

Then if we really know and can find our place,
God will forgive us our mistakes by His Holy grace.

Then no more lives on this earth will we need to span,
And we will return to God, by His own hand.

In Your Hands

You are your master to make yourself what you will.
You are your master your destiny to fill.

It is all within you this power to use,
To do great things, yes, even abuse.

The God within you is at your command.
To use it wisely you need only to understand.

You can then lift yourself above the crowd,
And clear away that blinding mental cloud

That keeps you shackled and unknowing,
And the God within you only dimly glowing.

To tap it, to use it, and bring it in full play,
You only need to believe in yourself day after day.

Yes, believe in yourself and the power that be,
And a wonderful change in life you will see.

A change that can only be for the best,
If others you help and your selfishness you let rest.

Throw out your arms and set yourself free,
And know of God that He truly be.

Know that in your way no man can stand,
For your destiny is now in your hand.

All things before you become your tool,
As you enter this wonderful inner school.

Control your body, throw out its fears,
Control your life, its very years.

Hold out your hand to those who need,
This, my friend, I sincerely plead.

For you have reached that point of all hope,
You have reached that wonderful upward slope.

Yes, it is all within you, this wonderful thing,
And because you have found it, closer to God it will bring.

Understand

See the good in your fellow man,
Look at each soul and find what you can.

For in man is that beautiful spark,
And in his soul sings the song of a lark.

We do not know what trials each one must overcome,
We do not know what in the past he has done.

We do not realize by an act of kindness,
We might fan to life his spark of fineness.

We only look at some unfortunate soul and quake,
And with indifference say, "His bed he did make."

This could well be very true,
But how do you know his bed wasn't made through you?

Some day you may well need
Someone desperately your problems to heed.

Then when you find there is no one there,
You will wonder why nobody cares.

If each of us could only see
That kindness to our fellow man must be.

Then understanding would spread like a raging fire,
Consuming mankind's selfish desire.

With man then understood by man peace would prevail,
And man would move toward his goal without fail.

Not Ours To Have

To desire something that is not ours to possess,
Can bring us havoc and to our lives distress.

It can become the overwhelming thought in our mind.
All else falls to the side and our true course hard to find.

It makes us unhappy and unpleasant to be around,
As we drive ourselves relentlessly for a thing not to be found.

It tears at us from our very head to our very toe,
And fills our body with misery, with pain, and with woe.

We feel sorry for ourselves, because to us it has been denied,
And unshamed, our desires we cease to try and hide,

Never thinking that for us this thing was not really meant,
And it was truly a test of our lives that God had sent,

A test to see if we have progressed enough, you know,
To take our unwanted mortal desires and them overthrow.

If now we could be free of this useless force,
We could head ourselves down our intended course.

Not really caring what others may have or own,
For happiness, you see, in possessions is not shown.

Thoughts

If all thoughts were put into deeds,
What kind of world would we live in, I plead?
For many a good thought into deeds never make,
And if all bad thoughts were deeds, this world would quake.

Now all thoughts need to be kicked around a bit,
Before a place for them we can find to fit.
For many an action taken in haste
Only gives to us our time in waste.

Many a thought put into words too quick
Can make us wish our tongues would stick.
Then there are those whose thoughts are good,
But never speak out when they really should.

We do have a problem that is quite plain.
How do we put our thoughts into deeds that are sane?
How do we make the most of what we think,
And still keep from stepping over that brink?

If we really try for thoughts that are pure,
With the help of God they would come through, I'm sure.
Then we would know what good thoughts to use,
And bad thoughts would disappear, we would not have to choose.

If all thoughts were put into deeds,
What kind of world would we live in, I plead?
For many a good thought into deeds never make,
And if all bad thoughts were deeds, this world would quake.

The Merry-Go-Round

The merry-go-round is full of fun for those who like to ride,
Whirling in a circle upon horses stopped in mid-stride.

To the beat of stirring music the world goes flashing by,
And for a ride that is free, the brass ring everyone must try.

Whirling round and round with the wind upon your face,
Your imagination joyously takes you through time and through space.

You are now riding happily through meadows and through glen,
Or charging down a mountainside where the air is pure and thin.

But all too soon, as you really knew it would,
The music comes to a stop and your steed turns to wood.

Your dreams they all vanish and you are filled with doubt,
And you wonder if your life is like the merry-go-round's circular rout.

Are you always climbing on some happy, joyous ride,
And getting off where you started, gaining not a single stride?

Are you always reaching for that shiny new brass ring?
Never realizing, when you get it, only another circular ride does it bring.

The merry-go-round of life goes nowhere now you see,
It only goes in worthless circles carrying with it you and me.

There is no easy way for the problems of life to overcome,
We must mount life's mighty steed and ride straight ahead toward the rising sun.

The Unknowing Sleep

Man in all his greatness is fast asleep,
That what he really is is buried deep.

For man went to sleep eons ago,
And forgot what he is, where he must go.

They tell us that from animals we sprung,
And we are climbing higher rung by rung.

But I am inclined to think it is the other way around,
From greatness we have descended toward animals, down.

But now I hope we have reached the bottom of our fall,
And we can start climbing back up before on all fours we crawl.

Perhaps this may be a bit absurd,
But man must wake up and remember the teachings he has heard.

Before he can gain even one inch of ground,
Before meaning to his life can be found.

He must shake off his schackles of hate,
Which are only a part of this numbered earthly state.

He must push away his selfish desire,
Which is only of his flesh and burns him like fire.

Of others he must most surely become aware,
And not with unseeing eyes at them stare.

He must raise his eyes to God above,
And then know the true meaning of the word we call love.

Then and only then will he awake from his long, long sleep,
And the full knowledge of life from his depths shall leap.

He then can turn back to his fellow man,
And say, "May I help you? Follow me, take my hand."

Courage

We are told with courage all situations to face,
If we show fear it will surely bring us disgrace.

We are told courage comes from being physically strong,
And if we back away from danger we won't last long.

Now courage is a great attribute to possess,
And without it this world would sure be in a mess.

But courage, like many things man tends to misuse,
Like many things of his character, it he does abuse.

He says it is courage when he commits aggression,
And courage he claims when he hauls down another's possession.

Courage he bellows as he wipes out an enemy's ranks,
Then in blasphemy turns to God and gives his thanks.

Do not misunderstand the lines I write here,
For courage we must have and hold it dear.

We must have courage every day of our life,
To help us overcome this mortal strife.

We must have courage every day we live,
So we may develop and of ourselves give.

We were given courage so we may open our eyes,
And with our courage toward Him we may rise.

The Pessimist

O what stirs inside you, my pessimistic friend,
What drives you to speak words that cut and offend?

Is there no beauty in life that you see?
Must you look and condemn all that is around thee?

Is there no way to reach the goodness that is inside,
That you have pulled into a shell and there try to hide?

Is it because you feel life has given you a bitter pill,
And you can stand no more of this, you have had your fill?

If this is true just cast your eyes around,
O my pessimistic friend, there are so many more worse off than you to be found.

I know, my friend, you feel others, too, cut you down,
With words that hurt and actions that you feel are not sound.

But remember this, if you blast others with words of hate and dissent,
Those very words back to you will surely be sent.

And your pessimistic views will envelop you like a growing black cloud,
Then only you can disperse it, with the love you are endowed.

It is there burning deep within your heart,
Relax, my friend, let its flame have its start.

Your Day To Make

You must learn each day with hope to face,
Never breaking your stride or slacking your pace.

You must face each morning, the dawn to greet,
With a stance that is firm on your two feet.

Yes, greet each day as it is something brand new,
Looking forward to its promises it surely has for you.

Expect each day to be the most joyous in your life.
Do not even think it holds struggle and strife.

Look forward to each day with an excited anticipation,
And you will find you can conquer most any situation.

Expect the day to be full of friends you will meet,
Perish the thought there may even be the slightest of deceit.

Hold the thought this day no problems will bare,
And if one comes up you will quickly and easily handle it there.

Think of each day as a positive thought,
And of the negative, very little will be wrought.

For each day is mostly what you make,
And if it was unrewarding it was probably your own mistake.

Look For The Good

Dear God, may we look for the good in others us around,
May we seek only the goodness that must abound.

If we could only look for that which is pure,
Then we could understand much more, I'm sure.

We look so hard for that which we condemn,
And we seldom notice the kindness within.

Let a man falter and we damn him at will.
We so seldom extend our hand to lead him uphill.

The next time you see someone you want to denounce,
Look at him closely before you pounce.

Look at him hard and look at him true,
Before you say, "With you I am through."

For the good in each is duly recorded,
Find it, my friend, and you will be highly rewarded.

Silver Sands

Man has risen to his greatest heights and fallen to his lowest ebb,
He has had moments of sheer glory and hours of hellish dread.

His existence upon this earth has been like a rolling ocean wave
That washes sparkling upon the beach's silvery sands, only to fall back
    to its watery grave.

Like the mighty ocean man is surging, struggling through,
Seeking, searching to find a place to flow into.

But unlike the mighty ocean man above his waves can rise,
He need not fall back from the silvery sands, if he listens to the wise.

For every wave of man that washes upon the silvery beach,
A few do cling on and higher ground they do reach.

And as they stand and watch the procession down below,
They raise their eyes to God and pray all men will know

That on the beach's silvery sands all men can find their long sought glory,
If they will only remember God's beautiful old, old story.

Sing Us A Song

Sing us a song, they said to them,
Sing us a song of man's wants and whims.
Sing us a song of joy and fun,
Sing us a song as bright as the sun.

They raised their voices clear and smooth.
Their harmony was perfect and many it did move.
They sang songs of the things of man's life,
His love, his happiness, his troubles, his strife.

Their singing moved those who heard to great delight,
And many stayed and listened throughout the song-filled night.
For singing strikes the strings of man's heart,
And sets his soul free and his woes fall apart.

For singing seems to blend man with his fellow man,
And the harmony created causes man together to stand.
If we could only look upon life as a beautiful song,
Then look for the harmony, when things go wrong.

Like the flowing notes of music, we listen to and sing,
The harmony of life, to us great heights can bring.
If man could only his discords cease,
And just once raise his voice in harmony, he could find his peace.

Sing us a song, we must say to them,
Sing us a song of man's wants and whims.
Sing us a song of joy and fun,
Sing us a song as bright as the sun.

Doubt Not, Fear Not

If we are plagued by fear and doubt,
And if our uncertainties we scream and shout,

Truly the fault within us lies,
For we refuse to think and open our eyes.

We decide this or that is to be feared,
And we draw up our defiances all highly geared.

We rush around and make ourselves all upset,
Without even knowing the reason as yet.

We work ourselves up into a terrible state,
And our fears and doubts we readily relate.

As we run about and denounce what we don't understand,
We bring pain and hurt to many in the land.

The things we fear and doubt we try to erase,
Never dreaming we could destroy that which we cannot replace.

It seems we do not want to think the problem out.
We only want to eradicate that which we doubt.

Destroy what is new, destroy what is old,
Destroy all that upsets us, many this thought hold.

Never thinking, never wondering, never turning to God,
As we crush great ideals, as ever fearful we onward plod.

We are ever ready to destroy and condemn,
O my God, your son, we destroyed even Him!

Time

Man is shackled by time through all his life,
He is mastered by it through victory and through strife.

From its ever passing he cannot run,
And its demands he can never, ever shun.

In his work and daily life it presses without relief,
And weighs on his heart heavily in time of grief.

Everything he owns and everything he loves must go with its passing.
Nothing in this earthly experience is everlasting.

He struggles with it in an ever losing fight,
And only in sleep is he free from its overpowering might.

When he awakens he finds he must be on his weary way,
For time is there challenging him for its race of the day.

If it is true that this earthly life is hell,
Then Satan himself must ring time's unholy bell.

But man in the end will be the undisputed winner,
For time cannot follow man when into heaven he does enter.

Friends

Many a person in our lifetime we meet,
Many a person we give a smile and say, "My friend, I greet."

Of those many people we casually refer to as friend,
Oh so few are our friends until the end.

For a friend is someone who with you will share
Life's goodness, life's badness, all with an understanding air.

A friend who will always beside you stand
Is worth more than all the riches of any land.

For friendship is truly from God a gift,
Cherish it always and do not cause between you a rift.

Understand your friends as they understand you,
Open up your heart with loving kindness too.

Say to your friends, "Here is my hand.
Let's march together through this life's stand.

"Let's march together as we have surely done before,
Let's march together in search of God's open door."

Talent

Talent is that which we can do quite well,
Though some have talent but choose not to tell.

Then some have talent and of it shout,
While others have talent but its value doubt.

Still others have talent and bury it deep,
Of others their talent comes while they sleep.

There are those who strive for a special talent all their lives,
But find it will not come but dormant lies.

Some use their talent for wordly gains,
While others use theirs to relieve man's pains.

You may say when it came to talent they left me out,
But believe me, you have a talent beyond any doubt.

Everyone has a talent to some degree,
You need only to recognize it, you will see.

Then use your talent to its fullest extent,
Find its use and to you what it was meant.

For God said of your talents you must give,
So you may progress and your soul may live.

Born In Sin?

We are told that in sin we are born at birth,
That our life from the beginning is a struggle on this earth.

It seems it is very difficult to understand,
How a seemingly innocent child is brought forth in sin on the land.

Yet this very thing may well be true,
If more than one life we must go through.

If we have lived many lives before,
We most certainly bring the sins of our past through our new life's door.

Our sins are not all we bring with us too.
We bring our good and our talents as we pass through.

You see, a newborn baby is not all good or all sin,
He is all the things of his past he has ever been.

With his sins and wrongs he has done in the past,
We must pray he will overcome them, defeat them at last.

Of his good and talents, may he use them well,
So in this life he may progress in the body he does dwell.

The truth of the matter we seem to see,
That born in sin we truly be.

We must do all not to push ourselves further down,
And strive for all we are worth to lift ourselves from the ground.

We must overcome the sins of our past,
Before we can reach our heaven at last.

Man's Destiny?

Won't we ever learn by our past mistakes,
Can't we understand what our history relates?

We seem to act as if this is the first time 'round,
Never looking back at the lessons to be found.

Maybe we can't remember our previous lives,
But our mistakes are written in history and here in record lie.

However, each generation will not read the facts,
And repeats its mistakes as if it were the play of life's first act.

We hear ominous warnings from a few farsighted souls,
But we head down the same ole path in spite of its woes.

Oh the scenery will be different and our society will advance,
But little will we do for our souls to enhance.

Will we forever be on this treadmill of time?
Is there no way for us the truth to find?

It is all up to us to improve our lot.
God told us how, we have only forgot.

To Sleep, To Dream

Oh sleep, what is your strange way, I ask,
What happens to us when at night we rest from our daily task?

What mysterious doors do you open that we fly through,
Mindless of time and space in whatever we do?

When we sleep, and perchance to dream,
Is it all just fantasy as it does seem?

Or do you, as in sleep we lie,
Give us glimpses with our inner mind's eye?

Can we by your seemingly meaningless flashes of light,
Perhaps gain knowledge, to life insight?

Ever since the time of earliest man,
We have tried to unlock your mysteries, learn what we can.

But perhaps this all is just a dream,
And nothing in reality is quite what it seems.

Perhaps, then, in dreaming we are really awake,
And see glimpses of our soul's existence, a tiny flake.

We may be given in our nightly sleep,
A small remembrance of a far off existence, ours to keep.

It is for sure as in sleep we doze,
We are cut free of our earthly pains and woes.

I am sure, too, our soul also needs its rest,
And as we sleep it slips away on a timeless crest,

Then goes out into a world to the mortal unknown,
To a place where there is no time and the seeds of dreams are sown.

Think

Think hard, my friend, think hard indeed,
Think to improve yourself, this I plead.

Think of others only thoughts of good,
Of how you want them to think of you, if you would.

Think hard, think long, and think deep,
Think of what you have sown, what you must reap.

Think, my friend, like you have never thought before,
Yes, think, my friend, of God's open door.

Think deep of life and what it really is,
Think of all the souls of the earth, they too are His.

Think deep, my friend, that God is real,
Think deeper, my friend, than only of your next meal.

Think deep, my friend, of Christ and what He gave,
Yes, think deep, my friend, before farewell you wave.

Be Thankful

Be thankful, my friends, of this wonderful day.
Be thankful, my friends, you are able to say,
   "I'm thankful."

Be thankful, my friends, you live in this land.
Be thankful, my friends, you are free from tyranny's hand.
   Be thankful.

Be thankful, my friends, as you sit at your meal.
Be thankful, my friends, hunger you do not feel.
   Be thankful.

Be thankful, my friends, of God's holy grace.
Be thankful, my friends, that He has looked upon this place.
   Be thankful.

Be thankful, my friends, that loved ones we seek.
Be thankful, my friends, that in happiness we meet.
   Be thankful.

Be thankful, my friends, your child's face bears a smile.
Be thankful, my friends, that in terror he does not cow.
   Be thankful.

Be thankful, my friends, you have been given so much.
Be thankful, my friends, for nowhere else on earth has God given such.
   Be thankful.

Be thankful, my friends, this you must.
Be thankful, my friends, but refrain from lust.
   Be thankful.

Be thankful, my friends, down to your very core.
Be thankful, my friends, then be thankful once more.
   Yes, be thankful.

The Star

The time had come, the earth was strangely still,
And those who were near felt apprehension, an expectancy to fill.

All was quiet and the star-filled sky spread over the low hills,
As shepherds tended their flocks, an art of their ancient skills.

The shepherds wondered why the sheep were so quiet and still,
And became concerned, thinking they may be ill.

But they could not overcome their own strange feeling inside,
They felt as if something was about to happen. Perhaps they should hide.

Then, as riding on the night-still wind,
Music they heard as faint as a thought within.

They stood and looked at one another, their senses beginning to doubt,
When in sheer terror they looked at the night sky and gave a frightened
   shout.

For the heavens had burst open with a brilliant light,
And a choir of angels had ended the stillness of that night.

The shepherds were so thrilled by the beauty of their song,
Their courage came back. They knew nothing could be wrong.

As they stood enthralled and bathed in heavenly light,
An angel came and said, "God has given you His son on this night.

"You will find Him in the city in a manger plain,
Go worship Him; He has come to relieve your pain."

The shepherds left their flocks, for Him they must seek,
And when they realized what had happened they became humble and meek.

As they walked toward the town of Bethlehem,
A brilliant star appeared in the sky and they knew it was for Him.

The Spirit Of Christmas

The spirit of Christmas is many, many things,
Joy, happiness, and bells that ring.

Smiles on the faces of children, bright,
Many colored lights shining in the night.

Friends gathering together with a holiday air,
Hearts opened up to those who not so well did fare.

A tingling excitement everywhere does reign,
And beautiful carols the world does sing.

The spirit of Christmas sends man in a whirl,
And for a few short days his goodness does unfurl.

He shows to the world his better self,
Then represents it all by a jolly ole elf.

There are those who would have us believe the spirit has gone astray.
This is not true as long as in happiness all do say:

Merry Christmas to each and one and all,
And may the blessing of the Christ on each of you fall.

His Gift Our Gift

Why did He come to us so long ago?
Why did He come to us only to suffer woe?

He came to teach man to save him from himself.
Yes, He came from God, no one else.

His coming was so great the heavens were ablaze,
And angels came to sing where the lowly cattle graze.

Those who came and fully understood
Knew this was the son of God, the true brotherhood.

As over the land the news did spread,
A wave of hope brightened hearts that were filled with dread.

For they knew this was the day,
That God had sent His son to lead the way.

Countless are the times this story has been told over the years,
And still its beauty brings to man's eyes a glistening of tears.

For man down deep wants to believe his life does hold hope,
And if he only knew all the teachings of Christ, with it he could cope.

Man is again now much like the souls on that night,
As they looked to heaven with awe and even fright.

For once again man's soul seems to be stirring,
And the light is creeping in, the truth is luring.

So make the most of this, the season of His birth,
Open up your heart, your mind, your soul; feel their worth.

Then go out and give the most precious gifts you can,
Your love, your understanding, your joy, your smile, and your helping hand.

Be Still

If time were only to stand still
And then perhaps I could get my fill,
Of things that in life pass me by,
For my days are so full to gain all I try.
It seems in great moments things I see,
Only to have them flee past me.
I am sure if I only took the time,
God would show me great truths to fill my mind.
It all is there for me to grasp,
I only need to take the time to ask.
If it doesn't come in one great flash,
I close the door and bring down the sash,
And then wonder why I didn't understand,
When God approached me with life's great plan.

War Or Peace

War! Men cry, we must save our land.
War! Men cry, they have insulted our stand.
War! Men cry, to preserve the peace.
War! Men cry, that nation must cease.
War! Men cry, we are at our best.
War men shall have 'til their soul is at rest.

Peace! Men cry, we want war no more.
Peace! Men cry, war is a terrible sore.
Peace! Men cry, it is for the good of man.
Peace! Men cry, for they say it is God's plan.
Peace! Men cry, for it is man's goal.
Peace men shall not have 'til it's in their soul.

The Flag

As we look upon our Flag as in the breeze it does wave,
We become aware of the story written on it and the burden it carries grave.

It is our Flag and for each and every one it does stand,
The great, the weak, the good, the bad, all that is in our land.

When you look upon it you see the story of people who desired to be free,
And the struggles that have and are taking place in this land of liberty.

It represents a place like no other upon this earth,
Where man can raise himself and find his true worth.

The Flag knows the story written on it is not perfect in any sense,
For the people who move beneath it at times are taut and tense.

But the Flag knows that freedom for all it does represent,
And with the help of God above, may the people turn from their pious bent.

May they understand that their Flag that waves above
Does mean freedom for all, guided by God's great love.

May they look upon it, with tears in their eyes,
For those who believed in the Flag so much, they gave their very lives.

May they see in the Flag not our nation's fault,
But the hope of mankind, and of tyranny the halt.

May they not blame the Flag for the wrongs that have been done,
For wrongs are brought on by man, each and every one.

Man has not learned truly how to be free,
But the Flag represents freedom's school, let us learn from it, yes, you and me.

The Land

Terror came upon the land and anguish filled every heart.
Where once there was peace, dissension now tore it apart.

The people were torn and looking for the cause,
And ranted at their leaders and blamed faulty laws.

They wanted those in power to bring back their beautiful peace,
With laws and edicts that surely would make the torment cease.

But all the laws and edicts that man could contrive,
Could not end the restlessness that across the land did thrive.

Something was amiss, something that no one quite understood,
And to seek and find what was missing, it didn't seem as if they could.

For what was lost was from each and every heart.
They had lost their understanding, O such a tiny part!

Then they lost a speck of love for their fellow man,
Just enough to keep them from raising a helping hand.

This did not seem to be a loss to only one group,
But all across the land it fell with a mighty swoop.

No one really understood what the other was all about,
And every group looked at the other, with fear and with doubt.

All were torn apart and chaos reigned supreme,
As man fell farther and farther and forgot his beautiful dream.

Who could save this land from its seeming fate?
Only each finding what was lost, before it was too late.

For each to turn to God and pray to be complete,
Before this beautiful land fell upon itself, in a rumpled heap.

Satan's Song

O listen to me, you men of the earth,
Listen to me and I'll fill your life with mirth!

Do not worry about the things you do,
Do whatever you want before your life is through!

If you must crush others so you may reach the top,
Get right at it before on you they hop!

For no one really cares about how you feel,
And they will laugh in your face if on your knees you kneel.

They will call you sissy and think you a bit odd,
If you go around saying that you do believe in God.

Really now, I say, what has God done for you?
Just look at the mess things are in, he sure didn't follow through.

So I say to you, just let me lead you by my hand,
And I'll make you master of all this so-called God's land.

I will shower you with riches beyond your wildest dreams,
And I will make you powerful and in all supreme.

And his I will give to you, and you need not worry how you act,
For this is the least of my conditions and is a known fact.

All I want from you to fill your life with bliss,
Is the soul from your body and this you'll never miss.

For you are not even sure a soul you have got,
And you are not aware whether it is around or not.

So what cheaper price could I ask you to pay?
I will give you everything for something you could easily throw away.

God's Song

O listen to me, my children of the earth,
O listen to me, and seek your true worth.

Truly I say to you, you are really all mine,
And in your flesh surges a soul true and fine.

I constantly watch over you and at all times ready to help,
As in your flesh you struggle valiantly in your attempts to develop.

It hurts me deeply as far away from me you fall,
But just realize your mistakes and I will forgive you all.

For you are on this earth for many things to learn,
And you must overcome many problems before to me you can return.

O please remember that life is your soul's great school,
And for it you are living. Let not your flesh of you rule.

For your prison of flesh lasts only such a short while,
While your soul is in eternity and blessed by my smile.

But your prison of flesh can last life after life,
If you continue to pursue only the ways of mortal strife.

Please raise your eyes to me and take my hand,
And let me lead you back to your intended stand.

For I am your father, your one, your all.
Seek me out and I will help you return from your earthly fall.

The Meeting

God and Satan, they had met somewhere between heaven and hell,
And Satan was telling God that his fallen angels were not doing so well.

Satan sat there smiling and chuckling with glee,
And said, "The way things are going I'm sure I'm winning them all for me.

"Just look at your creation, they sure are a sorry lot,
And if you think I'm kidding, my fires are all red hot.

"Now remember, God, ole buddy, you have got to admit,
That nine-tenths of your fallen angels aren't even worth your spit.

"And if you think I'm just going to sit around while you give them
    another chance,
You'd just as well go fishing or to some wild earthly dance.

"I really don't see why you even waste your time,
For even you must admit that they all are acting like they are mine.

"How many lives have you given them to find their way back to you?
 I really think you are a fool for I would have told them long ago I was
   through."

Now Satan was feeling boastful and figured he had tied God's hands,
And went right on ranting and raving and telling just where he stands.

"Really now, God, the trap upon the earth I set,
Was really a dinger and I know you it did upset.

"When your angels settled on the earth and found they had to stick,
I laughed myself near silly, then laughed till I nearly was sick.

"Then don't you think I did real fine when I made them forget who they are?
And they lowered themselves to just above the animals, and above that
   not very far."

Then Satan doubled up with laughter, in all his hellish mirth,
And pointed his finger at God and laughed, "Your son, they even purged
   Him from the earth."

Now this was about all that even God could take,
And He was about to grab him and through his devilish heart drive a stake

When from down below a single voice was raised in prayer.
It was pleading to God for forgiveness for all people there.

God then looked at Satan and said, "My unholy friend,
As long as there is one soul who believes in me I'll fight you to the end.

"As long as a single person prays for all the others down there,
Not one single fallen angel can you from me tear.

"For I have one weapon with which you cannot compete,
And that, my son of darkness, is love, and it spells your defeat."

Satan paled and managed a feeble grin,
For he knew the truth God was speaking and it made him quake within.

He started retreating to return down below,
For he had pressed his luck too far with God, this he did know.

Then God's voice boomed and followed Satan all the way down,
"Your days are numbered, Satan, for soon the golden chains of love will
 have you bound."

Satan returned to hell his wounds for to lick,
And this time it was not hellish laughter that made him feel so sick.

The Fallen Angel Wonders

The world seems to be changing so fast I can hardly keep the pace.
At times I wonder if it is worth it all just to stay in the race,

Or should I just sit back in my years not too old,
And meditate on things of the past, and the wisdom of many that we hold?

Should I be content and say, "The devil must have his fare"?
Or should I get right into the thick of it and help cut down the devil's
 share?

How can I say I will forget this world and its fateful run,
When every single one involved in it is of God, yes His very son?

How can I say it is all entirely too much for me,
When all around me there are those who are falling and reaching out, don't
 you see?

How can I back away from this world and its rapidly changing way?
I know now I cannot, for with it I must stay.

I must give what I can with all of my might,
To help this changing world to move toward the father and His Holy Light.

The Awakening

    Man stands on the hilltop and observes himself,
    Then looks around and says, "I'm above all else."
    This perhaps might be true,
    If man really looked at himself through and through.

But man, somehow, does not live up to his domain,
And it is apparent he has foiled his given reign.
Man has forgotten he is of God,
And through celestial beauty with him has trod.

Man has forgotten why he is here,
And the lessons of life he fails to hold dear.
He now through life rather blindly treads,
Cursing God for the woes upon his head.

He doesn't realize these woes were wrought,
In his lives of the past and long forgot.
He doesn't understand this restlessness in his soul,
And pushes it down because he doesn't know.

He shrugs his shoulders and pushes it away,
And hopes it doesn't return to cause him dismay.
But return it will to disturb his mind,
And there those who the truth will find.

Then it will burst forth like the rising sun,
And man will know he and God are one.
With peace and beauty he will stretch his arms out high,
To return to God with one last earthly sigh.

He has now returned back to God,
And knows full well why on earth he trod.
He knows truly this is his real domain,
And gladly says farewell to his earthly reign.

The Aquarian Sunrise

Time has swirled endlessly since the beginning of man.
In many ways he has learned much, but little of himself does he understand.

He now finds himself in a highly developed state,
Master over all except himself, which is sad to relate.

But as before this pinnacle he cannot hold for long,
Unless he masters himself and builds a soul that is strong.

Cracks in his accomplishments are now beginning to show,
And can only be shored up if he allows his soul to grow.

Man talks much about the dawning of a wonderful new age,
But at times it looks more like the dawning of a new outrage.

Then still, before the dawn, the blackness reaches its peak,
Perhaps now those who believe in God and man should stand up and speak.

Yes, stand up and speak and help man through his darkest hour,
Before he turns on himself in a disastrous shower.

Hold out to him understanding, love, and hope, all in your hand,
So together with he and God in the new sunshine you can stand.

Now, hear his melody as if it were floating on the wind.
But this time you will know it is the music that God did send.

You will know as Fallen Angels you will rise once more,
And the time has come for all to live as God had meant, on his now
    peaceful shore.